Last One Gone Turn The Lights Out

By Ray Tempus

I0793493

Last One Gone Turn The Lights Out

Published by
One Temptation Press
545 Eighth Ave. Suite #401
New York, New York 10018
onetpress@yahoo.com

www.40points.com

ISBN: 978-0-9772587-2-7
First Printing: 2007

Acknowledgements

Being the reclusive and introverted grump that I am I like to use this page to tell the few people I'm lucky enough to call "friend" that I appreciate them. Sherry, Rodlyn, Jenna, Margarita, Punkin and Anthony may as well be family. The family gets a holla here too. (Hay! & I'm O.K.)! Love to all the X's even though you must all be crazy. Special thanks to my friends; Christine and Barbra for almost single-handedly keeping my work relevant (sculpture), Robert Malfi for more than everything, Kennedy Moore for a stage. (askanewyorker.com [#1 NYC website]), Dana (painters need inspiration), and Doug Ward at 1TPress for making this happen. When in that place termed; "in the wheel", where a; "body of work", is created, be it paintings, sculpture, books, music, or whatever. One finds ones self focused on the project to the point where 25 hours a day "working" just happens. Coffee becomes blood and your blood becomes coffee. I developed a radar for Starbucks. No eye contact just a growled, "grande coffee no room". But one day a pretty smiling face looked up at me and said, "hi, I'm Janette". Whew! Friendliness still exists, and Starbucks seems to have found all of the nice people.

Became a daily routine to sit, have a cup of coffee and write, or shall I say rant a few pages. (Hey, the place has atmosphere). It also has some other nice people; namely, Selene, Shannon, Lydia, Pooja, Makeisha (wink) and Mary (who is the meaning of adorable). While you all brighten up my day, you're ruining my grumpiness and I thank you for your hospitality. I didn't forget Shawn or Enox, but ladies first. Now I gotta go and wean my self off coffee. A special shout out to the boy's at, "Cheers"; Tulio and Santiago for keeping it real. Thank you Hattie Hightower for getting the party started. (wink). Everyone's journey is a best seller, you just gotta write it down. Then comes the hard part. ('smile').

Table of Contents

Section 3

Section 4

Section 5

Welcome to the World according to your crazy uncle who is kept on the back porch.

Introduction

Last One Gone Turn The Lights Out

By Ray Tempus

I'm going to the Beach! I'm taking my easel and I'm going to the beach. I'm taking my easel and I'm going to a nude beach. Now! How ya' like that! I win! See ya' later baby. Before my couch candidacy became a noticeable, 'rubber room', need. Complete with little rubber ducks and non-toxic crayons.

Allow me to apologize early if anyone get's offended by the contents of this; 'just for the record', rant. This is not my intent. May I suggest you take nothing personally, too seriously or literally. (wink) BUT, I'm only the umpteen thousandth person to come to the point of exhaustion with the madness. What madness? It's all madness. If what passes for pop-culture is any indication, this thing is broken. Hmmm.....popular culture?

The reality of the word popular becomes mortifying when coupled with the word culture. Because any "culture" no matter how sophisticated or un-sophisticated, is constantly developing by It's very existence. The fact that things are going backward is obvious to everyone and everybody's talking about it. Yet we're too busy to focus on the tiny building blocks that separate us from the dark ages.

In our current society the nobleman has no place unless his nobility brings wealth. Any ol' lowlife is praised if they've got a bundle. It's like a giant bait & switch. A three card monte, pea under the cap. They'll sell you snake oil and give you your change in three dollar bills. Corporate theft, I.D. theft, petty theft, internet scams, stock scams, charity scams, exploitation, sexploitation, polluted farmland, polluted water, polluted air, polluted airwaves, polluted minds, polluted mouths, racism, sexism, fascism, totalitarianism, scumbagism; lies, lies, lies, lies

lies!! Where does it all end? I'll tell you where. It doesn't!

Though I do believe we were making progress in leaps and bounds for a while there. Made everybody in the world want to come here, rich or poor. It still works, I don't deny. You can still go from rags to riches which is kind of the point here. Not just materialism. I'm talking wealth. Real wealth. Comfort and joy wealth. Financial security and then some wealth. Let your money work for your wealth. Lifestyle plus accumulation, wealth. Yes! This is still the land of milk and honey. Making it? Yes! Keeping it? No!

That's why the corporations have their headquarters off shore. By the way, a small business is a rich person not a mom & pop shop. Those small businesses that do off shore banking are individuals that make a bundle and instead of moving to Florida move to the Bahamas. No income tax, no capital gains tax, no inheritance tax. The national slogan is, 'It's better in the Bahamas'. The biggest buildings are not the tourist resorts or casinos. The biggest buildings are the Swiss banks.

Our best and brightest ain't paying taxes folks. Even the companies who's revenue comes directly from tax dollars don't pay taxes. They rent a P.O. box in Amsterdam or an office in Dubai. (see Halliburton).

But the whole thing seems to be becoming a captive corporation. A better version of those 'Captive Market' Banana Republics where your money is only kind of your money. Try taking it out.

While you can still get it out, you gotta get it out. Here's why, once you can't get it out and it could happen, the whole market economy will become like a big Cracker Jack Box. A cheap surprise. The saying that goes; the only things in life that are sure are death & taxes, will become the national slogan.

Take the money and run! Later in the book I'll list some of the best tax havens to run off to. Stable economies, (thanks to your money), great weather, beautiful property developments and beaches. Now I won't tell you how to make all of the money necessary to escape to paradise, I haven't quite figured it out yet. (that's QUITE, and YET).

Don't look for any how to books once I do. Those grinning 'how to' book authors/sellers make their money by selling you the book or tape or seminar or whatever. If the stuff in the book actually worked they'd spend they're time doing just that. They'd be so stinking rich that they wouldn't need to travel around with those silly stories motel to motel, all so that "you" can enjoy the happiness and freedom that they now do. Snake oil! It's all snake oil.

Now remember I said quite and yet. The title is "Last One Gone Turn The Lights Out". Yet, no how to books. I'll have no time. Beach BBQ's take time. Sand sculpture takes time. Painting sunsets take time. Girl watching takes time. That's right. Girl watching, I'm a guy. What do you expect.

Besides to say Last One Gone implies that I'm leaving you behind. I am! You and the government. If before mentioned entities can profit by our tax dollars and move to avoid paying taxes on these profits; I'm not sending them damn near half of my money. I only contribute into the tax base. I get nothing from it.

Besides my money will do a lot more for me than it will do for the government. It'll grow twice as fast if I have twice as much. And I can buy lot's of cool stuff. The government will just buy mobile homes that no one will ever live in.

I could go on and on but I don't want to create meandering musings of a semi-madman. As mentioned these pages contain a, "just for the record rant", element. An, "I saw what you did, and I know who you are". A, $!#@ the government kind of thing.

The omni-present reflecting seems somewhat a confessional, it's not. I've nothing to confess. Seems tatle-tail. It's not, there's nothing to tell. These are the things I encountered along the ' yellow brick road'. I'm saying that the great and powerful is just a little man behind a curtain selling a big lie to all the people in the land. (and collecting taxes). Not necessarily a bad man but when you look closer a very bad wizard.

These are not memoirs or any type of time induced life crisis stuff. That'll come when I get tired of looking at those damn waves rolling to shore the same way over and over everyday. But that will take a long long time because the girl watching thing never gets old. Better keep a NYC summer home. Just in case.

Peel through these pages and you won't disagree. My dues have all been paid in full. Since I love you I just thought I'd let you in on a cool idea...... O.K., I don't love you; but you feel me right.

The times of writers block I experienced while struggling to complete this book's self-imposed deadlines caused great anxiety until I realized it couldn't be writers block because I'm not a writer. I am a painter, I am a sculptor...........ok so I guess I am a writer. I'm kidding. I am a

Painter/Sculptor. Writer? I bought term papers.

The bound antidotes such as this and my "A 40 Point Guide To Peeing In New York", are books in make-up. So by extension I'm a writer. Or, better, 'Author'. Only in America.

Now, why am I leaving?.....Read on.....

GOOD-BYE
TO THE BEACH
TO THE BEACH
GONE FISHING
Last one Gone Turn the Lights Out!

Section 1

(un-coothness)

Chapter 1

Table Manners,..... or better (the Lack of Table Manners)

...and this, after you invited me for dinner. Not to be snobbish, but poor table manners disgust me. First things first; left hand fork, right hand knife. This is not a lesson in technique, though it is quite important. Just let me say don't lace your fork between your fingers and hold it food surfaceside up like a tiny shovel to scoop the food maximum load. Let the knife assist the fork. No fingers. Bring the food to yourself, don't go down for it. Don't reach for your food with your tongue. When having soup or other spoonables, spoon away from yourself. Always use your napkin correctly and watch the elbows. Now; enough of the snobby mechanics. This is about more offensive behavior.

Check this out for yourself. Whenever you go to a restaurant to dine, rather you're at a five star or a seen better days grease bucket. At some point during your stay some nasty-ass is going to pull a snot-rag from their nasty pocket and while at the table blow their nose. Loud!!

Real nasty like too, uck! Though in this setting there is no un-nasty way. Now this person or persons may not be done eating at the time of the offence, but either way one should excuse oneself to the restroom. Going outside would be o.k. except in the bathroom you can wash your hands. This disgusting act should be punishable by a long period of wearing a, ' I'm a booger swallower', T-shirt.

Also, isn't talking while leaning toward the table kind of yukkie. Many people spit when they talk. UUGGHHH! Those specks of flying food. UGH!!

Lean back in your chair when it's your turn to talk. First swallow. Don't talk too loud, use mild hand gestures to help. Never clear your throat. If it's a classy restaurant and you're hoping to make a good impression on your dinner companions don't order anything that you pick up with your hands. (except bread). Reasons for this are numerous. And women shouldn't order meat. Especially the meat that when you're done the poor critters bones are left on your plate. Maybe that's just me but it looks like such damage was done. And there you sit looking fulfilled. Scary.

Things to never do when at the table.

There will be No.....

. Ear picking
. Nose picking or touching
. Scratching
. Coughing
. Hocking
. Throat clearing
. Snorting
. Loud laughing or Talking
. Leaning on the table while talking
. Food in mouth talking
. Nasty Talking
. Kissing
. Volume burping
. Stinking
. Tooth picking
. Farting
. Easing out of quiet farts
. Hair Management
. Finger nail clicking, (ladies..... I hope)

- Facial Hair touching, (fellas..... I hope)
- Sneezing
- Sneeze stopping (run away)
- Drooling
- Yawning
- Elbows on the table (oldest rule in the book)

Awful things you can kind of get away with.

- Easing out a silent burp is kind of O.K. as long as it doesn't smell.
- Dozing off is o.k. if you're leaning back in your chair and are balanced.

While it tells your boring company that they are in fact boring, you can do no more harm while sleeping. Unless you slobber or a fart jumps out.

I can't help but re-call one puzzling dining experience. Two companions and myself found ourselves in a summer resort-town café in the winter time. Luckily we were the only patrons. Because I would've hated to have been with;

"those ill mannered city people". Who even come to ruin lunch in winter.

The other male in our party received a call on his cell phone. We had already placed our order so to be polite he went outside to take the call. Our food arrived so we had the person attending our table to cover his food. My friend and I proceeded to dine. Her gracious table manner didn't surprise me, as she is a cultured and tasteful woman. Luckily we'd finished our food before our other companion returned. After being outdoors for nearly an hour he came in sat down, uncovered his plate, took out a snot rag and blew like a foghorn. Why didn't he do that outside? You sadly shake your head.

After that one I won't even mention the classy gentleman who looked the casual professional young grandpa. Classy, 'that is', until he took his index finger and used it as a utensil. Digging into a large cup and scooping out the contents, then licking and sucking his fingers until the next enthusiastic dig. The guy went at it like a crazed maniac til the very last drop. Then licked his hand for several minutes.

But after those nose blowers this crazy guy doesn't even warrant our attention.

Chapter 2

Lemme get

Lemme get. That's where it all started. ....Kinda. Point Being general acceptance of small breakdowns in manners and grammar in it's un-coothness is contagious.

Bodega's or Boutique's; from penthouses or cardboard boxes. Get to the counter and it's blurted out, whispered or whatever; "lemme get". Education level doesn't matter, social status doesn't matter, walk of life or economic level. No matter. The person ahead of you, or ordering near you will answer when asked or just blurt out, "lemme get".

Tourist, immigrant whatever. The only English phrase people seem to know is lemme get. Tell me it's not just me. If it doesn't happen to you then you're the one in front of me. Either that or I am walking through some evil parallel dimension. Because it drives me crazy.

It's not lemme get. It's, ' may I have' or 'I'll have', or ' I'm having', 'give me', 'ABC', if it's a nameable product. There are a thousand correct ways to respond or ask for something. Lemme get isn't one of them.

This may sound like nothing, but it's that constant drip that erodes the foundation. Eventually you've got real structural problems that take greater measures to stabilize.

I've come to the reality that general manners are still possible and improved social graces could happen. But something as sophisticated as passable table manners is a bit too much to expect. And it's all because of lemme get. What next? Now were seeing. All sorts of unimaginable nasty's are accepted as casually as lemme get.

Loogie hocking is the most disgusting extension. For those of you that are unaware of what exactly a loogie is, let me apologize before hand for turning your stomach. A loogie is the nastiest substance produced by the body aside from puke and pure snot. I think it trumps bile so by extension turds. To be exact a loogie is a combination of spit and snot; (mucus is just too nasty a word to use), hacked up from somewhere between the throat and the sinuses. Then violently spat onto, hopefully the ground, or even better the sewer. I say hopefully because you see em' everywhere. On walls, windows, subway and other stairs and handrails, door knobs, (this should be punishable by public flogging), phone booth's, bus shelters, etc. etc. UCK! And that's in the summer! In the winter..... I gotta stop. Now I'm sick. Maybe I'll be able to eat in a week or so. But you get the point.

It's gotten like lemme get. Everyone does it. I've even seen pretty, stylish women do it. That's worse than a crude dude doing it. And if that isn't awful enough I once saw a lovely young mother with her adorable little one who just as I passed hocked a nasty loogie on a department store window. Completely gave me the creeps. When she takes the little angel to the candy store the poor child probably says "wemme get".

P.S. I get those anti-smoking ads but..... they should be on at the same time as those infomercials. The same time as that smart-alec bastard asking you if you're drunk or high. They show the one where the scum is squeezed from the body part at dinner time. Who's responsible for putting it on then. You put the T.V. dinner people out of business. It may be effective but at dinner time? What kind of a booger eating sadist came up with the idea of showing that at dinner time?

Lemme get out of here. I'm going to the beach. No T.V.'s.

Chapter 3

Dog Walkers

Now I'm not speaking of the millions of normal folks with dogs as pets that accept the responsibilities of ownership. Nor do I speak of the countless hard working manics who trudge the streets with a dozen dogs in tow trying to make ends meet. I mean those, better than the rest of us prissy's whose dogs are also better than us.

Somebody tell lil' Ms. Thang she ain't looking so all that stepping Prada in your bag of turds. Pinky extended. You are as of now on the level of we peons that you pee on. All because you bent down and picked up a hand full of do-do. Stinky! Stinky! Stinky!

It kind of turns my stomach to see someone stooping down to actually gather turds. That smell! It's even worse to see it in the winter. Because when it's cold outside you can see smoke coming up off of the turds because the do-do is fresh and warm. UUGGHH. That really looks nasty! You can just see the horrible stink.

That's why I can't own a dog while living in New York City. I flatly refuse to pick up turds. That's Nasty.

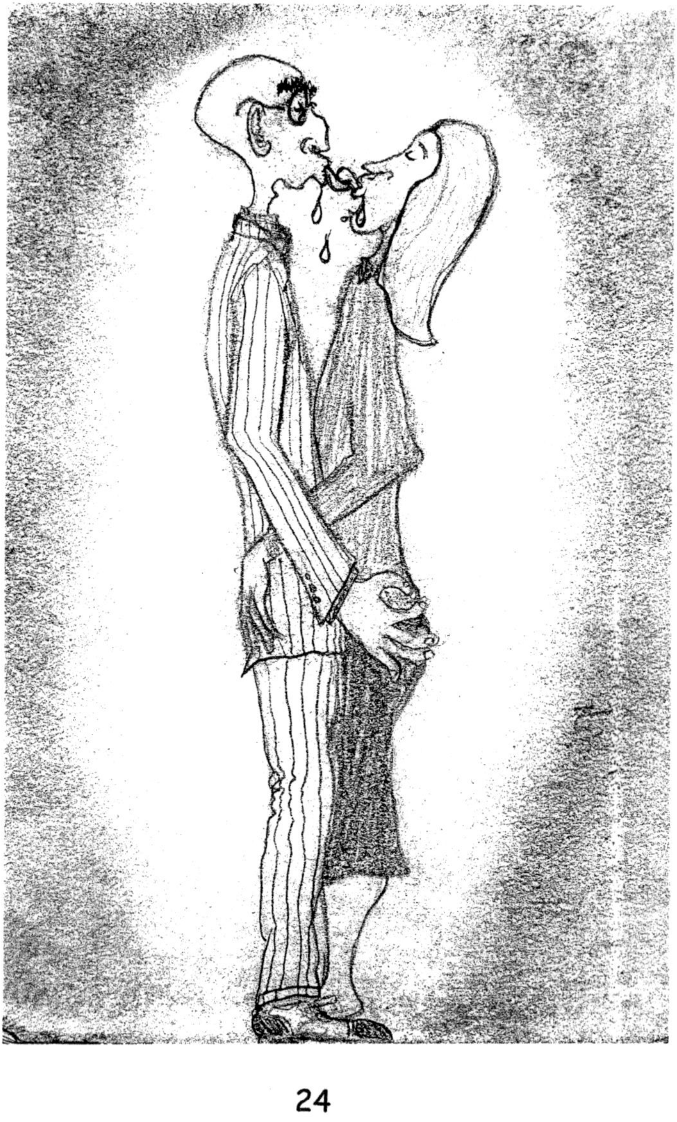

Chapter 4

Overly Affectionate Couples in Public (Wet Kissers and Booty Grabbers)

You know those couples that can't seem to keep their hands off of each other in public? You know the ones. ....The wet kissers and booty grabbers. The ol' get a room line isn't enough. We're here to say what needs to be said. And that is; stop acting so high school! We don't care that you finally found each other. Why do you think it took so long? Nobody wanted either one of you, you're both ugly. O.K. let me stop being mean. But stop being so insecure you're making us all sick.

Of course this isn't the only puke provoking behavior of these, (look at me) couples. There's all kinds of awful stuff. Imagine this... True Story, I'm on the subway one Saturday evening. 8 o'clockish, good weather so the trains are full but not crowded. I was standing near the doors holding on as the train was in motion. Seated 15 feet or so from me was a young couple sharing a fun day, and also sharing a huge lollipop.

Now this is no ordinary lollipop. It was at least a foot long. Only about a third of that was the stick. The lollipop part was a long colorful hard candy. A tube like cylinder, tightly and neatly twirled around the stick.

The pretty young female held the lollipop. She had long beautiful hair and apparently one of those long beautiful hairs had twirled around the lollipop. Upon licking cutie noticed the hair. She pointed it out to her beau, who lovingly took the hair between his thumb and index finger. He then un-winds, or I should say un-twirled the hair. UCK! UCK! UCK! The hair is beautiful when attached to her head. It's downright disgusting wrapped around that damn sucker! Because of the sticky on the hair Romeo couldn't really discard it.

A young woman playing a computer game of some sort sat in the seat next to the door at which I was standing. Two feet or so, from where I stood. She too noticed this nasty event and was uckied out about it just like I was. It made us both sick. We momentarily bonded in disgust. I offered quiet commentary, to her

DOWNTOW

approval. The offending stink pot couple just went on taking turns sucking the contaminated lollipop to my and my temporary compadre's repulse.

Now if not for the accumulative effects of this healing rant this would not end at uckie disgust. It would be reason enough to never take a subway or bus again. As a matter of fact, be it not for this therapeutic exercise I'd probably have a difficult time ever going outside again.

Come to think of it,....

Chapter 5

Commuting

By train, by bus, by car or walking commuting is a decent into hell. And the evil of which I speak has taken over it. Not unlike what happened to that lil' girl in the Exorcist. It's taken over the voice. Sounds simple but it's in the language. (see lemme get). One fundamental change has occurred. The commuter used to be, "The Passenger". Now the commuter is, "a customer". Sounds trivial but the change was a conscious one and changed simultaneously among different agencies.

The Government drinks bile. Now to the immediate problems. By car; traffic jams, bad drivers, road rage, nowhere to park,..........all annoying. Gas prices can make you opt for public transportation, Public Transpo? Oh Hell! The government doesn't even make you swear and they're trying to kill us all.

While buses have many of the same road

THE FACE OF COMMUTING
NO IMAGE
NO IMAGE

annoyances as cars, it's to a greater degree. In my city if you're in a hurry you'll never get there on time. Crazies are a problem but they seem to prefer to ride the rails. And every nut in town is always on the way nowhere and they take the train. Every beggar, every thief. Pick-pockets are nothing when you have to worry about knife wielding maniacs. Rush hour, you are a sardine. Packed in with who knows who, breathing out who knows what. Influenza lives! UCK, somebody has gas. I'll walk.

Walking combines all the problems and consider you gotta dodge the cars, the same crazies plus the ones that have no fare money and air quality is so foul you can see and taste it. Bikes, blades, segway's ect? You figure it out.

Section 2
(Totalitarianism)

On ISMS

First let's define the isms in every day speak:

<u>The cow analogy</u>
Which system are we?

1. Socialism- If you have two cows, you give your neighbor a cow. (O.K., but...)
2. Communism- If you have two cows the government takes both cows and you <u>might</u> get some milk back. (let's leave or be lazy)
3. Fascism- If you have two cows, the government takes both cows and shoots you. (how'd we get here!)
4. Anarchism- If you have two cows, you steal another cow and shoot the government. (this is a result.)
5. Capitalism- If you have two cows, you sell one and buy a bull. (this could work)

Chapter 6

The Government and Politicians

The government is trying to kill us all. May as well just get to the point. Really! They want both cows. (apply appropriate, "ism"). And what is with this, "Rock Star", promotion of those seeking our approval in the form of votes. They in turn use the same appeal to promote the agenda's of the diabolical cow thieves promoting them.

Hmmm. ...... The political arena? Now there's a parallel universe if one exists. A place where down is up, balls have corners and three dollar bills are tossed out like vote for me buttons. ' Network' time. You know; "I'm mad as hell and I'm not going to take it anymore."

As of this manuscript I ask for your assistance in the formation of the, NARV movement. (N.A.R.V.; Non Affiliated Registered Voter). Whom among us can be defined by a single ideology.

I'M GOD.
VOTE 4 ME

I propose we do away with group membership. The Boy's and Girl's thing; we gotta keep that one. (for restrooms). But in reality all of the other divisions are applied to us. Let's pretend we can all think for ourselves. (Now I'll be labeled an Anarchist or something). Just label me crazy. (That only broadens my latitude for behavior).

By the way, the only reason I'm not running for President is that my heart is set on sun-soaked beaches and off shore banking.

Capitalism ain't totally dead yet. I said YET! Forget new cars and vacations. Quick, buy a bull put your little cows on e-bay. Then take the money and run .

If you don't think capitalism can die check two factors. Check out the recent changes in the patent laws. It doesn't matter if you re-invent the wheel. If you ain't rich the wheel government will own you. You get a certificate, but guess who keeps all of the money.

Secondly check out democracy. It's dead! Murdered by stolen elections. Last one gone turn the lights out.

P.S. "Election Improprieties" or stealing elections is akin to a passive overthrowing of a Democracy.

Chapter 7

Homeland Security, Police Stateism

Homeland Security? Our safety depends on the U.S Department of Home Land Security? Uh-Oh! This is a humor book so I won't mention the recent history that validates my uh-oh. And uh-oh is putting it mildly to say the least.

If in fact some groups or governments were really gonna do us in the department of Homeland Security couldn't stop it. Remember they're responsible for securing our borders, you see how that's working.

While watching CNN one afternoon I saw Homeland Security Chief Mike "chicken-neck" Chertoff being asked by The commentator how the department knows how many people were illegally crossing the Tex-Mex border. He seemed taken aback by the question. He nervously responded, " well um, one way we um, check is by um, footprints".

You gotta be kid n' me. While the response is among the stupidest things I've

BUSH-LADEN UNIT
HOMELAND SECURITY

ever heard, the fact that these idiots don't prepare better for what they'll obviously be asked is just as ridiculous. It's not surprising because they aren't prepared for anything. They couldn't fend off an attack by turtles.

But fear not, no one is coming to get us, and if you believe they are you'd better head for the door even faster than I'm running.

Oh, and about the guys in the armored vehicles that periodically step-out in their silly looking helmets and scary looking M-16's? Theatre!! Who the hell are they looking for? They don't have a clue.

However I did observe them in action once. An officer in the K-9 unit spotted a helpless homeless person with all they're worldly possessions in a small plastic bag sitting on the floor of a train station. He leapt into action! Commanded the dog into attack mode siccing the dog on the poor woman, all teeth bared. But to his credit he never let the dog get closer than 8 inches to her TERROR filled face. And I'm sure he meant no harm because he and the small

JUSINO
COWBOY

group of uniformed NYPD police officers (3 or 4) laughed hysterically the whole time. I guess they were just seeing what it would've felt like if they'd been able to go to college and be real frat boys. And what's with the army guys. Theatre! But continuous Theatre. Well at least if they're here they're not in any unnecessary danger.

Maybe they should take over for the police department. At least they use their tax payer bought uniforms. The police department seems to think 90% of the force should be undercover. So, are the blue jeans, the sweatshirts and sneakers they wear on the job everyday tax payer bought?

Where are our uniforms? And where are the squad cars we paid for? Buying a whole fleet of raggedy-ass cars that now litter the streets and not using the new fleet of high-tech squad cars seems foolish for many reasons.

First of all who doesn't know that the shitty looking cars with blackened windows and a group of "teens" joy riding are cops. The out of state plates don't fool anyone either. Nor the taxi cabs. How many twenty-thirty something chaps with the " I'm from Long Island look", drive taxi cabs with a buddy in tow? ZERO!

It's cute that their communication equipment looks like popular every day electronics. Those I-Pod looking ear phones are cool. But about the cars. I thought that the police department and all city vehicles were taxpayer purchased. Aren't they required to be U.S. manufactured cars. Not foreign made cars like the Nissan's and Toyota's with blackened windows. The Chevy's and Chrysler's with blackened windows are at least U.S. vehicles. The taxi cabs are also U.S. made cars.

These guys also don't fit in. They're not cosmopolitan enough for Manhattan. They look too trailer park. They stand around trying to look casual. Fit in. They look like they can't wait to get home to tell their mommy how their day on the big job went. These poor guy's earn less than a tin-can collector and not only do they have to police, but now they're occupied with acting like they're not policing.

The result is now they look like stalkers.

FREIGHT DOOR

All to justify ridiculous hours of overtime pay. And what's the advantage in trying to hide the police. So criminals will go ahead and commit their crimes and get caught by the cops hiding in the little ugly car with blackened windows? If the knuckle-head had known of the police presence he wouldn't have violated your property or person. Wouldn't you rather see those crime deterring cars and have the perpetrator get out of the vicinity than have the cops hiding behind blackened windows but catching the guy after the assault of self or property.

It's police-state thinking. Over policing. Make em' think danger lurks. Everybody seems more paranoid of late. Like everything needs to be guarded and watched. Enter; THE SECURITY GUARD. Every building, every lobby, every store, everywhere. If this is necessary it's all gone insane.

By the way. If your family came over on the Mayflower and you chose a career that pays less than a 15 year old illegal immigrant earns in tips delivering pizza? You too, should think of leaving this madness. May I suggest lotto.

P.S. ; As a tax payer I'd like to know if the guys on the bicycles wearing maroon T's or jackets that report to the undercover guys are on our dime. I know they're immigrants, probably illegal immigrants. It's fine for them to work but not on taxpayer payroll.

Isn't police entrapment illegal? The department captain who supervised an entrapment scheme should be jailed. Get this; this person had carts of groceries left on the subway platforms so that someone thinking they'd found someone's cart that had gotten on the train and forgotten it; then responsibly tried to turn it in to the station agent, only to be arrested for theft. If this is not illegal, a police state is lurking.

I'm not sending tax dollars to paint windows black. I'd rather buy fresh coconuts and banana leaf hats.

Chapter 8

Reefer, Reefer Madness & Mad Cow.

Marijuana makes you a lazy fool. While you are under it's influence only!! So There!
We just stated marijuana's most extreme problem. The next biggest problem is, you ate a whole pie.

- Don't smoke weed before homework or studying for exams. You'll get stuck on stupid.
- Don't smoke weed then go drive the car. Your perception of depth can be a little off. And those fast approaching objects can pop up out of no where when slightly tripping.
- Hide the car keys & the twinkies.

Why regress to the insane reefer madness days. I don't think that even the crazy neo-cons can repeat some of that madness though I wouldn't be surprised. They've already started the propaganda but the truth is marijuana does not lead to drug use.

It was a time when it was said that it transformed " Negroes ", into crazed animals that play anti-white satanic voodoo music. And they were talking about Jazz. Can you imagine what would've been said if rap had been around then? The truth is somewhere in the interest of the industries that would be adversely effected by the production of industrial hemp. Not the strain of hemp with the potent flowering buds.

I'm not saying to smoke weed. But wouldn't you rather see college kids and young adults pass a joint than a bottle. Lets be honest and compare. Neither is good for homework. Period. Neither is good for driving, but booze is a million times worse.

Puff a dube, you wanna listen to the radio until you're inclined to raid the fridge. Take a sip and you want to hop in a car to go raise hell. Get a group of young people together passing the bong, they order a couple of pizza's and some ice cold coke; listen to music, laugh at nothing, denounce the government and laugh at nothing some more. O.K. so the nightclub didn't make any money. Give the same group a couple shots of booze; time to go "out" and have fun, Bud's driving. Though the odds have decreased, let's pray they all get back safe.

The car isn't the only thing that could be hazardous. Drunk people are so obnoxious, they'll pick a fight with other drunk people or sober people. But the other obnoxious drunk people are more willing.

The land in jail factor, the land in the emergency room factor, the land in bed with who knows what factor, the puke factor. And let's face it; women's problems can be even more frightening.

I mean, college kids gather and smoke pot, then sit around and talk philosophy. College kid's gather and drink, then play dangerous games or go out and damage whatever. Just for fun. But it's back to the days of reefer madness.

To mildly poison yourself is o.k.? Alcohol is technically poison. Think about it. Drink it and your mind and body functions change dramatically. You walk crooked and the next day you're sick as a one eyed dog.

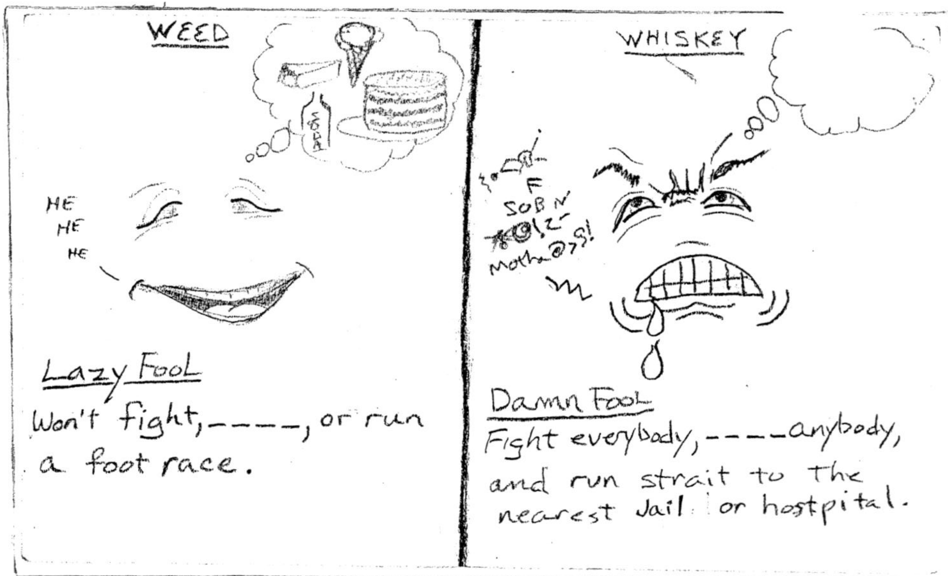
WEED
HE
HE
HE
Lazy Fool
Won't fight,----, or run
a foot race.
WHISKEY
F
SOB N'
Damn Fool
Fight everybody,----anybody,
and run strait to the
nearest Jail or hostpital.

Puking on anything in your way. You've been poisoned, though be it mildly.

But I really don't have any fear per se. It's the other propaganda that concerns me. Besides you'd have to have mad cow to believe that weed will kill you.

Hmmm? I wonder which one of those tax haven governments I can bribe into allowing me to farm hemp on my land. Industrial of course.

P.S.

This is a postscript example. The actual scene took place after this chapter was written. This happened one evening while sitting in a Pub/Restaurant in midtown Manhattan. You could call it popular but there's an unmistakable yesterday feel. Almost a nostalgic element to the place. In the early evening 6 to 9 o'clockish 30% or so of the patrons, (like myself), are there to dine. The chef (Tulio), is the only guy left in town to offer seconds at no charge. The bar is lively and they have half a dozen or so TV's with sports playing. The old regulars give the place a neighborhood pub feel, the other bar people make the place a real dive. This particular day as I was watching a basketball game, a commotion broke out at the end of what was not a crowded bar. One guy picks up a stool and clobbers another guy with whom he argued. He then pummels the poor fellow to the floor and beats the stuffing s out of him. The young lady tending the bar, (very pretty but a don't let the beauty fool you vibe), rushed over to pull the guy off. Another patron stepped in and slammed the beater to the floor, although I believe cutie could've handled the deal. That guy then leaves threatening the guy he'd already beat up. The guy that got whipped was helped to his feet. He ordered another pitcher of beer.

He and the other guy had been drinking together before the beatdown. The guy who got beat up; that's the second time I've seen him get hit over the head with a large object by the person he'd been drinking with. Wanna tell me this guy shouldn't stay home and smoke a joint.

BAR
NO SMOKING
CRAZY
XXX
XXX
IGNORANT
OIL
DRUNK
ACT A FOOL
FOOLISH FOOL

Chapter 9

Corporatization

Done! Look around. You can't beat em'. You gotta join em'. And it's a natural product of capitalism. Forget about mergers and acquisitions, Airline and Automobile manufacturing. Let's talk about the everyday stuff.

Gone are the days when you could open a little family business teaching the next generation how to carry on. No more Sam's Sandwich Shop, or Bill's Burgers. You gotta buy a Subway's or McDonald's, or whatever franchise. Wanna open a little print/copy shop with internet access? May I suggest you use the same sign colors as kinko's. If you're lucky maybe they'll buy you out and hire you.

Corner store? Nope. Ice Cream parlor? Nope. Shoe store? Clothing store? See the Gap and all the other like stores owned by the same corporation. Coffee Shop? Don't even think about it. You can't possibly make coffee as consistently delicious as Starbucks.

And their competitors be damned.

Pizza parlors are the one thing that's been ruined by all of this. Because each pizza making family has it's own recipe. None can be matched by bulk production. Enjoy what's left of the real pizza parlors before they're all gone.

As I mentioned the real diabolical evil of corporatization is not ground level visible. They also have a much more profound effect on our lives.

Cottage industry entrepreneuring is not just alive but thriving. The internet creates a million opportunities. And some types of businesses that have always been there for the hearty souls willing to roll up their sleeves and work 25 hours a day can now make more money than ever before.

Personally I love day-trading and Texas hold-em', But I'm not talking about or suggesting either. If you can find a way to make a hobby profitable you've got a chance to prosper happily.

Remember, these corporate mover and shakers actually enjoy the diabolical stuff they do. It gets em' off. Proves there's a devil. And proves my point. A franchise is like an over-lord that super-taxes you for the rest of your franchise life.

Lotto's only a dollar so it's not the worst gamble, however if you're the type with a little swagger and would like the very best card counting method for casino blackjack that exists, contact me through the publisher and for a small fee I'll share it with you. It's perfectly legal but you'll be asked to play a different game or should I say not allowed to play blackjack once you're suspected of card counting. Our way of life is being devoured by the monster. Culture?

Well, you know where to find me.

I reluctantly confess that I won't be at all disappointed if the beach bar serves Starbucks Coffee.

P.S.

Don't sell little cows generation after generation. You sell your cow, your bull and the future generations of little cows exponentially. A cow pyramid so to speak.

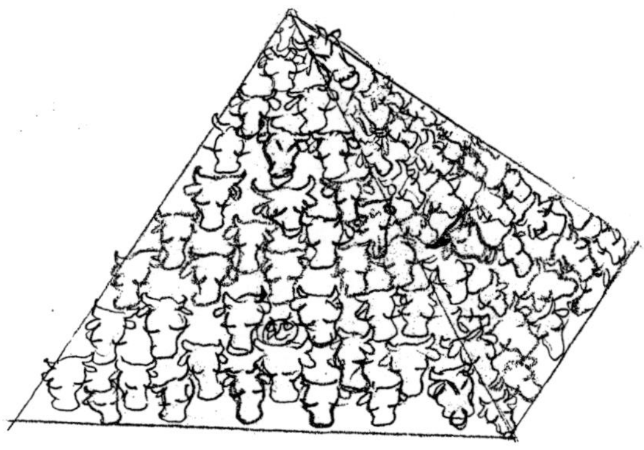

Section 3
(where are the cops?)

Chapter 10

Wall Street (My First Career)

My first image of the big Stockbroker/ Trader/ Investment Banker or whatever, was probably what many people imagine. Corner office, mahogany desk with high back leather chair. A couple of phones, couple of secretaries, box of stogies to offer. Calling the market and cutting big deals. NOT what happens!

The desk & chair you get, though not the big deluxe type. You also get to share whatever electronic system is being used to monitor the financial markets. You quickly realize that these are niceties above what the brokerage firm believes necessary for your success.

The telephone is the one thing you will surely get. You are a telemarketer after all. And phone you must. 100 calls a day 200? I know of a situation where if you were not on the phone selling, they'd take your chair away. Now I'd definitely pimp slap any tyrannical fool who'd try such a thing. But you didn't hear me say that. (one, two, three, four, five.......etc).

My business cards said Investment Banker. Wow! I called myself a stockbroker. Technically I was an account executive. Whatever you call it, it's a glorified telemarketer.

Now, true there is an awful lot of money to be made when you are, "GOOD". But what is good? Some would think that good means you make money for your clients. That isn't necessarily what good means.

The house doesn't care if your clients lose every dime. Good means the same thing it means in any telemarketing or sales job. Dial more and sell more. By hook or crook.

Regulations are strict and defined as to what's legal. Cross the lines no problem, just don't get caught. You look around and find yourself not only in a den of thieves, but you yourself a lying crook if for no other reason your total lack of understanding of the business that you are in.

I couldn't take it! I'm too honest. I was one of the good guys. At least I'll admit I was a crook.

I didn't start off a crook nor did I mean to be a crook. It just kind of evolved.

I wasn't a lowly stock jockey the whole time. I started out a legitimate trader of precious metal mining companies; meandered through stock exchange equities & options, a little futures and commodities trading. Then I ended up in the slimy, grimy world of penny stocks.

Then I managed to go even lower into penny stock promotions. But at least then I was only pushing the crap off on the lying low life brokers like myself.

And to think, if it had all been a few years later I could have skulked into the lucrative world of those totally unregulated hedge funds. Now let's see, they're essentially investment clubs for rich people only and they're not regulated. Gotta be crooked. But since I don't speak on things that I don't know about, I'll get back to the thieves I lied with.

You only need to know of this one situation to get a macro view of some of the shenanigans. I was once Affiliated with an, " Investment

Banking" firm that publicly underwrote the corporate stock of a company who's product to market was a cocaine snorter. No, I'm not kidding. True story. Now this may in fact be my own colorful description, but what's in a name. The company didn't call it a coke snorter. It was called a nasal applicator. It's purpose was the nasal delivery of pharmaceuticals.

They reasoned, laboratory test's had proven taking some drugs nasally was more effective due to higher and faster absorption than ingesting. They claimed to have gotten FDA approval for one or two drugs to be delivered nasally. So they manufacture a small short plastic tube with a small matching plastic tray. Why not just a rolled up dollar bill? Nothing will convince me the idea didn't come from sniffing cocaine.

Now as for the underlying stock. What a scam! The offer, or the buying price began at .01 cents per share. At that time the bid, or selling price was ½ of .01 cents. The offer, or buying price went up to $1.00 the bid price at that time was stated to be .50cents. Now I know that you are thinking if you bought the stock for .01 cents per share and you can now sell it for .50cents per share, your profit is phenomenal. Even if you get it at .25 cents you've doubled your money. Keep in mind this meteoric rise was in just over a year.

WOW! Yeah, that's how it looks from the outside. Problem is you can't sell the stock. You can sell it,...... but. Selling one share will drop the bid to 1/10 of .01 cents and that's what the remaining shares will sell for. Sounds crooked huh. I know that's the way it works and they get away with it. It's only unethical, not illegal. It's only despicable.

I don't need to offer anymore examples but I will mention that the same group took a company public that was, a guy with a couple of popsicle carts around the wall street area in summertime. Raised the guy 1.3 million dollars to make popsicles. But, he got new carts. Hmmm? Kickbacks? Nah.

Oh yeah, the popsicle guy had formerly been a crooked stockbroker. Many former stock guys create little companies and go public. You get to play with a lot more of peoples money and legally spend it on yourself, and remove yourself from that daily grind. It's either go public with something or face this as a daily routine. After the "blazaa" morning; coffee while phoning, meeting, phoning, more phoning, coffee, phoning until lunch time.

Then the most amusing ritual occurs. A large percentage of these young executives head outside to meet their, "weedman", $10, $20 whatever. Puff a joint grab a snack and go back to the office and repeat the morning grind.

Now the reason I brought this up is because of the obvious backwardness of the wall street recruiting process. The wrong people are employed. It doesn't take long to see that the poor, mis-educated, $300 a week weed seller is miles ahead in the hustle, quick thinking, work ethic and business acumen necessary to be, "remember good", at the stock selling business than the $3,000 a week mama's boy's that are legally stealing. And at day's end, let's all go get drunk.

Then of course you have your nasal delivery crew. And they ain't snorting Dramamine. I don't know which group is bigger but they're both big. And looks can be deceiving. (Case in point). Think of what is stereotypically considered the all American young ivy league MBA look. A guy I once worked with fit that description perfectly. He knew how to use it to his advantage. He was in reality anything but. The reason he thought just snorting cocaine was "ok" was because of the three day, free-base cocaine smoking binge he'd once gone on. In his office mind you. Started on a Thursday afternoon, continued through Friday. Day three, Saturday? Hate I wasn't there to see it. The guy ended up on top of a building damn near naked proclaiming to be Jesus Christ. Then on to the funny farm, with belted coat.

When they turned the fool loose he came right back to work. Same office, same desk, same chair, same tasteless wise cracks. Hey, he was "Good", for the firm. And at days end let's all go get drunk.

If you combine the weed for lunchers and the tooters, the number pales in comparison to the drunks; I mean drinkers. They talk shop over cocktails every evening. Then consider you got boozy weeders, boozy cokers and everything goes-ers. And at day's end, let's all go get drunk.

I have no reason to mention the ordinary smart people that have productive honest careers in the business. That would show how lucid and sane I really am. Then I wouldn't be able to get away with saying these things.

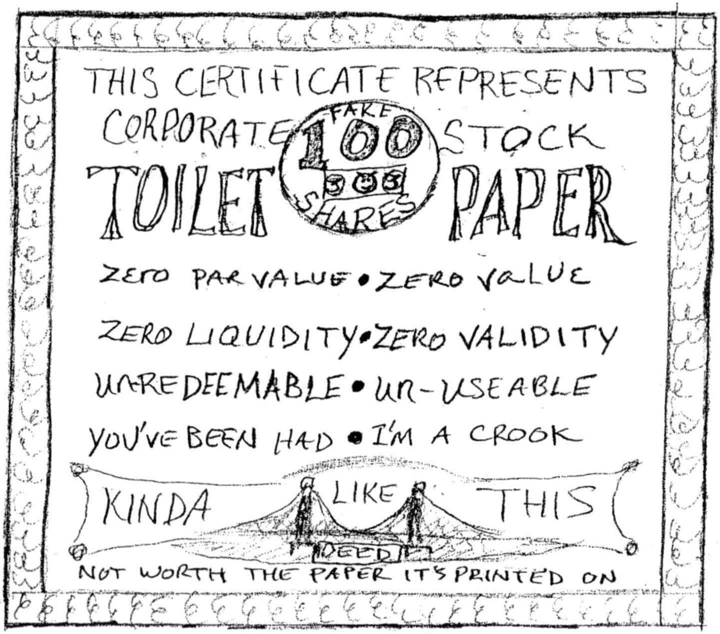

Chapter $10\frac{1}{2}$

Part 2 Entrepreneuring and Spying

I set out on my own entrepreneurial trail meeting crook after crook along the way. Not always crooks but seedy Amway types. But first I hung my own shingle so to speak.

I offered, through national advertising my professional services for those seeking high risk venture capital. I thought it would be an extension of what I'd been doing. Figured I'd be good at it. Figured wrong.

I was so bad at it in fact, that it seemed as though I was a real crook. While I did get a couple of deals done, (2), none of my other clients (and their were many) got a dime. They just poured money down the drain that was me.

My intentions were good. I was just totally disinterested and really lousy at it. My upfront fees were to be deducted from my commissions that never happened. I mean the being owed commission part never happened. I got the up front fees.

So I moved on to a new business that I was accidentally good at. I advertised locally my services as a spy. I ran simple newspaper ads that read;...I spy (_ _ _) _ _ _-_ _ _ _. The first call I got was from a group of young lawyers. They had gotten involved with a new 'business associate'. He was an older gentleman and did not practice law. He was an investment professional.

They had invested a load with the guy but weren't so sure that he himself had the means to put up his part. Because he and his, 'wife /secretary' moved their operation into the lawyer's offices they felt a reason to trust. They were hoping the guy's story as well as his investments were legit.

Their suspicions led them to hire me. Go figure. I had two lunchtime meetings with three or four people at which time we laid out a plan. I was to come up to the office as if I were a client of one of the attorney's. This would give me the opportunity to take away documents and view the suspects and more importantly, their files.

Now the name of this "partner", was never mentioned at the lunch meetings. If it had been I would've worn one of those Groucho Marx noses to disguise myself. As soon as I opened the door and took one step inside I recognized a woman working just behind the reception area. The "wife". Luckily she didn't see me. I backpedaled right out of there. I knew the woman and her, "husband".

I also knew in detail the crooked scams they cooked up. You see I was once a registered broker at his, (at first) legitimate investment banking firm. Through sheer crookery he turned it into his little piggy bank. He encouraged his young brokers to put the retirement funds of their clients into his pocket with a scam that was so big of a lie, he must have already had his bags packed.

He told those young brokers to get their clients monies out of those "illegal", 401K's and Keogh plans. Put that money into "his" private placement. By the way the "wife", wasn't his wife. She was his girlfriend.

EPTION DESK

I'd be surprised if he wasn't planning to drain the real wife of whatever they had and run off with the girlfriend.

At the brokerage firm she was called his personal assistant. And this was no mid-life crisis of some former all-American throwing it all away for some hot young gold digger. The guy was an old gray, wheezing, fat slob. She was not as repulsive as him, but she wasn't much better. No, these two were true to each other. Partners in crime, united in thievery. Ugly soul mates.

So after practically running out of the place. I immediately telephoned the client and summoned them to the lunch spot. (might as well eat). In the next hour or so I explained in detail everything I knew about those two. All of the holes in their crooked story lined up.

Think these young esquires were impressed with my genius? They've probably christened their yachts, estates and second born children in my honor. They didn't even have to pay me, I was so elated to deliver that dastardly S.O.B. ....o.k. they had to pay me. But you get the feeling. I felt I owed the creep.

They also referred my services to an associate. For what he needed I would've had to actually know what I was doing. So I didn't take the case. Then some poor guy hired me to spy on his wife whom he suspected, and correctly so of cheating. I didn't have the heart to tell the guy. Couldn't crush him like that. I knew the only honorable thing to do was to leave the profession. (laughter).

Somewhere in between all this action; we'll just call her "Natasha". True Story!! I mean we're talking Russian accent, raspy voice, stunning beauty, Rodeo Drive Chic. ... No cigarette holder. (hey, you can't have everything) She called and requested a meeting. I'm thinking she wants to hire me, however she wanted me to hire her.

You think I was gonna tell her that I was a clueless kook? I'm no fool. I'm 007 and then some! Gotta spare you the details because I wouldn't believe it myself if I hadn't been there. (Only in the movies).

That always lurking devil-may-care side of me that's always up for a little adventure could be inclined to take one last venture into Spydom. Natasha's go nicely with sea-side sunsets.

Chapter 11

Snake Oil Salesmen

But don't just damn the gospel spewing phonies. Damn em' all. Cure all snake oil is on every street corner. Wall street can't hold a candle to some of the outrageous things out there. I actually know someone who was accused of selling swampland. That's an extreme. But, the more run of the mill stuff is plentiful.

The 501c3 fund raising organizations? All administrative expenses. M.O. have the dysfunctional staff people. (Administrators) council people that are even more dysfunctional. Or have the same otherwise un-employable staff offer employment advice to unemployed people, calling it an empowerment program.

Now these are the good people. Look at all the liars selling happiness and perfect sex. Hair and perfect sex. A licensed psychic, (whatever that is) and perfect sex.

Any merchandise that can be telemarketed in bulk will be conveniently shipped to you at a 2000% mark-up. Never buy: light bulbs, rubber gloves, tape, paper towels, toilet paper, printer paper, printer ink, copier ink, wrapping paper or perfect sex over the phone. These are bulk items. Sold at a premium. Perfect abs, super brain power, no more warts and perfect sex.

Then you get to the wealth sellers. You can own several income producing properties, no money down. You'll pocket tens of thousands of dollars at the closing and never have to work or worry about money again. So why are they telling anyone. Why not just go zap em all up? They tell you where to find em'.

I did buy a property once that I didn't have to put down any money. Everything else about the deal sucked! I didn't buy it through one of those shysters but I know why they sell the secret.

Continue down the alley and you get to the MLMers. The ones who actually have soap or whatever, aren't crooks, they just tend to be boring goofballs. Now the pyramid scheming MLMers are among the lowest of lowlife's. You'd just be surprised at some of the participants. The suspended wall streeters and real estate people are really no surprise if you've been around. It's the M.D's, P.h.D's, D.D.S., C.P.A.'s, ESQ's and these types who seek grimy mooches like themselves no matter their walk of life. Ax murderer, fry cook, shoe seller, clown; who cares? These people need a "down line" and if ya' got the loot, you're in. They're the ones that surprise you.

Then comes the, ('give used car salesmen a bad name') politicians. A lower form of life they are. When do they get under that rock they all seem to crawl from. Ambitious rich friends and a competent dentist are a must. Then they lie through those perfect grinning teeth so easily.

But everybody knows about them. They're bloodline is traced to lizards and they make a pact with the devil. But I know of one liar so outrageous that he even makes me say, "Where are the Cops"?

The case of the phony photographer. What this guy does is he goes around to frame shops where lots of inexpensive art prints and posters are sold. Many of the shops are owned by immigrants, south-east Asians in particular.

This crook get's photo-prints of 1950s and 1960s pop-culture icons. (James Dean, Marilyn Monroe and so on). He reproduces the photos on what seems to be a good quality digital printer. Still the quality is poor and pixilated. But, he claims to be the photographer, (I don't believe it) claims to make a limited edition and he signs them.

These hard working people want to strike gold just like everybody else. So they buy the story. They also pay this crook huge money. Then they tell the same lie to their customers who figure they know what they're talking about.

To sell this lie, and I only know of one guy he sells them to, he comes into the guy's

WOW!!
I'm a Crook

store with the "Xeroxes" in a briefcase. But before even "he" can touch them he must put on white gloves. He also tells them that they can have them appraised, but only at Sotheby's. And they need to make an appointment and wear a $2,000 suit to the appointment. So hard working people who believe in the dream must become lying snake-oil sellers to re-coup their money.

For the record, the photographer doesn't sign those type of photos to give them value. The person photographed is the one who needs to sign them.

The government offers the highest form of snake-oil. It's called propaganda. And, it's the greatest seller in the land.

I'm totally disgusted with the whole thing. I'm tempted to just sell my bridge and disappear to some quiet little safe haven,....oops I mean tax haven.

For Sale by Owner- Suspension Bridge, antique, stone & steel cable, seen in several movies. www.snakeoil.com.

Chapter 12

The Devil Totes A Bible

The Devil totes a Bible if you know what I mean. Not, Bible toters are devils. The Devil totes a Bible. And wears a sack suit. Liars, deceivers, diabolical plotters. The devil is in disguise. Clean shaven. Points to "the devil", to show you it's not himself. He says "see, its that guy".

Play's the save the children song and all the while a pedophile. Hypocrisy is so matter-of-fact. If, "I have sinned against you", then you ought to take ya' lying, lord praising ass into the smarmy brothel that is your mind and condemn yourself for stealing in the name of the lord.

Stoned junkies are on the airwaves denouncing drug addicts. Hypocrisy reigns supreme! The devil discourages individualism. Encourages uniformity to identify. Gotta be, "one of us". Gotta "look like us". Kind of in drag and I don't mean drag queens. The current says, "assimilate". "Ya' gotta

AH SWEAR I'M GOD
TOM'S MINISTRY
THIS WAY TO HEAVEN
HOLY BOOK
LIES

assimilate". Then reminds us to, "call in if you see those guys", you know the ones. Report any thing that's not in line with "us". "We won't blow your cover". "Tell on your neighbor". So what you've lived next to him all your life. ("Don't cha' see what's wrong? He wears red. We don't wear red. And what's with the whiskers? Where'd they come from? Probably smokes that funny stuff. We don't smoke it anymore. We weren't good inhalers anyhow. Uuhhh, "praise the lord". Hee hee').

Like I said, in drag. Bible and all. I advise you check for your wallet while Diablo e-mails his little friends.

I'm off!! My casa del sol awaits!

Section 4
(Telling it like it is)

Chapter 13

The Economy

Jamaica, needs to fix it's damn economy. The Jamaican government is the problem. I don't know the exacts so I won't speak on it except to say, corruption! What else could it be? Between bauxite, sugar, bananas, coffee, ganja and tourism. The economy should thrive.

Allow me to make a suggestion.....see Amsterdam! The warm weather, the beautiful beaches, delicious food, beautiful people, laid back atmosphere, the rhythm, the music, the mystic,......yes we come for all of the above. Now let's get real. It's the weed.

Tourist flock to your shores in droves expecting a spliff. You've been harassing and arresting visitors for weed and the word is getting around. People have already started going to your neighbor,(that I'll leave nameless), because "they" understand.

How does it help your economy to cooperate with this evil mandate for the

one for you
one for me

paltry sum of 2 million dollars a year in U.S. aid. This mandatory passport deal is going to put a big dent in your tourist trade anyway. No weed! Why bother.

Ask your friends of the Bahamas what a super tourist trade can do for your economy. Adopt the Amsterdam model you'll increase the tourist industry by 10 billion dollars a year. Can't you see it? Not coffee bars. Rum bars, beach rum bars with weed menu's. Hottest spot in the western hemisphere.

This is traded in for 2 million bucks? Who exactly pockets this 2 million? And why is Jamaica not a tax haven? Eliminate income tax and we'll bring all of our money. The wrong people are running the place. Implement these changes, damn the queen. You can thank me later. See ya' at sunsplash.

TREVOR'S
TREVOR'S MENU
GANJA
• 3 PRONG $
• RED BUD $
• SINSEMILLIA $
• LAMBS BREATH $
• SKUNK $
BEVERAGES
• SORREL
• JAMAICA BLUE MOUNTAIN COFFEE $
• HIGH MOUNTAIN SUPREME COFFEE $
• RED STRIPE $
• KILLER RUM $
• TING $
EATS
• ACKEE & SALTFISH • PEPPERPOT SOUP
• EVERYTHING SERVED WITH COCONUT WATER
• CHALICE OR HASHOIL ON REQUEST

Chapter 14

Part 1 Immigration
(I wanna be an Immigrant)

The rich kind who runs off to one of those tax havens with my earned, stolen or whatever gains. The reasons are obvious. Take a look at some of the places. Centers of Banking they call em'. Zero income tax. Zero capital gains.

Why do the Bahamas have Swiss Banks? Swiss Banks and Casinos. Tells you something. Add year round sunshine, Beaches & Junkaroo and you know where your stockbroker ran off to.

You see these governments speak a coded language through their tourist boards. Slogans like; It's better in the Bahamas, and come to the Cayman's.

Now they also mean to bring your lil' vacation dollars and honeymoon monies. But they really mean; here, hide it over here. We're not gonna tell. Bring enough and we'll make ya' one of our own. Begged it, borrowed it, stole it, we don't care. And check out the view.

I only mentioned the geographically closest ones. But I advise you do a google search for tax havens and find the right paradise for yourself. Offshore banking, offshore corporations and holding companies.

Some of, or at least one of America's most famous Real Estate Developers is building or has built a huge development on a tiny Caribbean island that I'll leave nameless. The reason I mention this is to show how it works. Buy a "High End" property in paradise and they'll make you a resident. The property these; "Investors", buy offshore will shield them from taxes and come with a tropical paradise estate.

The other reason I didn't tell you the name of the island is, I don't want to, " blow up the spot", for my future self or my future neighbors. And the beaches.

Sand sculpture sounds like a fulfilling hobby.

Cont......

Here are a few Tax Havens to consider, but do your own search.

The Commonwealth of the Bahamas:
No income tax, no capital gains tax, no inheritance tax, good weather. Damn!
I herby nickname thee, The Swiss Tropics.
/Bermuda(the shorts) /The Caymans /Malta /Anguilla /Antigua & Barbuda /Bahrain(if you're weird) /Cook Islands(you'll never be found) /Dominican Republic(surprise) /Panama(wow!) /Switzerland?; it's better in the Bahamas /Vanuatu: out in the middle of the ocean and they won't tell a sole a thing. This has to be the best. CIA operation cash transfers use this archipelago as well as White House voter fraud money deals.
Bingo!.....Hey, I just read the reports.

Subscribe to:
Escape from America Magazine.

Chapter 15

Education

There's no such thing as too much formal education. But no matter how much you have, you could come to a point of needing more. This need could be born of opportunity, or lack of opportunity. All J.D.'s don't work in the law profession.

I know one who is a practicing drunk. The bum tried to beat me out of money in a real estate deal. It didn't work because my idea was to cheat him. To his credit he did at least have his hands on my money. Although I wasn't in it for the money it was the properties I was interested in. Well I did get my money back.

But I'm getting off the subject. Back to education. You don't need to express horror at the situation with much of public education. Evidently the elite private school systems that later populate the, "best", universities are no better. This statement is based on the public figures we see today that hail from the "Ivy League" schools and other prestigious universities who are so obviously untalented. ...... o.k. stupid, morons, idiot's. It boggles the mind.

Now to be productive in the labor force you don't really need any education at all. None, zero. Just be reliable and willing.

I say this because a few years ago I was teaching English word pronunciation to Spanish speaking immigrants. (lots of Americans I hear speak could use the class). One of my students asked for private lessons. He had been working at a pizza parlor in the financial district for eight years. For just over a year he had been the manager. Dealing with the workers was no problem, they all spoke Spanish. He spoke English well enough to communicate with the customers because they were ordering from a menu that he was familiar with. He had a family and wanted to be able to help his children with school.

This was so important to him because he had never been to school a single day in his life. If he can manage a high traffic New York City restaurant without the benefit of a day of schooling or speaking the language it proves you don't need school. You need to be reliable and willing.

The poor unpopular kid from a broken home who couldn't cope and dropped out in the tenth grade is told his lack of education is the reason he or she is not employable.

Chapter 16

Part 2 Immigration..... and Immigrants

Immigration? Ain't touching it. Political jibber jabber and social divisiveness. I ain't in it. Immigrants? Gotta laugh at my friends. But first let me state for the record that my core belief is that anyone should be free to go wherever they want to go if the purpose is to improve their life.

Peoples of the Americas are pretty much the same culturally. A language difference is what it is. Comes around in time. A new town is a new town.

There's an underlying familiarity in general. People from Europe, Same thing. Western Culture I guess you'd say.

Now our friends from some of the more "repressive", lands around the globe? To go from a sexually repressed society to a sexually obsessed society. From where women are essentially kept hidden, to our self expressive stylish fashions. The backward opinions of the greater majority of people I've known over the years prompts me to defend the "GORGEOUS babes" of our culture. Wearing very tiny clothes and showing the world that you are, "to die for", means that it's 90°f in the glorious summertime. Not that they're; "not nice girls", as my obsessed repressed brothers seem to think.

They talk amongst themselves of how they have good women and the women here are sluts who go around having sex with people they don't even know. So they tow the line of seeking a better life all the while proclaiming there own homeland better.

They boast of family prosperity; doctors, lawyers, captains of industry and of course Kings. Yet they came for a "better" life. Who'd leave a medical practice to drive a taxi, or a law practice to work in a bodega? Who the hell would jump off of a throne, to mop up in a peep shop, which by the way is the nastiest, most disgusting thing anyone could ever do for a living. (Be a thief for crying out loud, don't mop up in a peep shop)!

Though they lie about their background the motivation is clear. They want freedom from sexual repression and other restrictive backward thinking. They end up replacing the repression with exploitation. Backward thinking causes this. They want to think "Western" women are loose and easy, instead of thinking free expression is normal. It proves two things.

1. Sexuality is a natural part of the human condition no matter where you're from.
2. A sexual relationship with no other relationship is either; Just one of those things (smile), way too much whisky or a financial agreement, which is usually exploitation. Often times of <u>very</u> young females.

My friends are serial patrons of prostitution and peep shop moppers. (I never shake their hands). I'll give you an example.

I got this little buddy from Bangladesh. And when I say little, I mean little. Claims to be all of five feet tall. He ain't a hair over 4'11".

He told me, (and I wish you could've heard it yourself), that what inspired him to come to America was the 80's TV series Dallas. In his own words; "I never miss an episode of Dallas cause I see sexy wōmen on the show. She bounce and bounce, so I want sexy wōman". "I come to America for sexy wōmen".

If you watched that show you probably know who he's talking about. There were a couple of cuties on that show. I just wonder how he thought 4'11" worked here. Did he know that actresses and model's and American's in general are kind of tall. I know a few tiny people from that region, I guess he didn't know.

This little fellow went on to tell me of his attempts to get a visa to come here. He kept being denied because he was too young. He was 17; you need to be 18 to get the visa. Instead of waiting a few months, he forged his brothers name to get a visa. It worked!

ASTING
FOR
DALLAS
SEXY
WŌMAN
STOP
HERE
POOT

So he packs up and heads for cleavage. He then went and claimed persecution in his homeland and got political amnesty. All this because American T.V. made the poor little fellow believe that tall, beautiful, rich, "sexy women" would meet his poor little sawed of ass and give him some nookie.

Now damn near twenty years later the guy can't get a green card. Without one he can't even visit home and return to the pretty good life he's built here. Here's a man who has no formal education that has built his own business from scratch, in New York City of all places. He owns property and all the trappings of the American dream. Problem is it's all in his brothers name. Let's just hope his brother never shows up.

The sad part is the sexy woman part never happened. So once the important things are taken care of, (mortgage, rent, insurance, etc). the rest of his money goes to beer, buds and hookers.

But he ain't like his peep shop-mopping homies, living 12 guys to one apartment and sleeping in shifts. So I guess we've proven the fruits of wrath can change a man's religion.

Section 5
($3 bills & keep n' it real.)

Chapter 17

Celebrity, Celebrities, the Celebrity Press and Celebrity Worship

Celebrity: root word, celebrate.

Who celebrates these people? Millions I guess. But why? Is it because they cure disease?....No. Is it because they bring about world peace?....No. Because they educate the youth?....No. They saved a baby from a fire?....No. Can tie shoes?.....maybe.

Our, "culture" celebrates actors more than the people they portray, who in many cases are great and heroic people. It's the Jesus syndrome. Worship the image of whom upon you spat. The drunkard trying to "act" like this hero not only gets public worship, they also get the money and the girl. (Change the gender if you need to).

Drop-out's they are. Drop-outs who ran away from the trailer park they call home. One pick-up from life at the truck stop. So now their drop-out spawns are anointed stars for no reason. Due props o.k., but worship?

Music makes the point clearer. Not what passes for music. Music. Played by musicians. The celebrity press knows nothing about them. I understand how it works. It's youth driven and kids don't know squat. But, must brilliance be a sub-culture.

Newspapers, magazines, TV, internet and every thing else makes sure the general population knows who won the Grammy, Oscar, the Emmy or whatever. But the Tony's (real acting) are backseat passengers. The real merit winners like the McArthur, Pulitzer or Nobel are mentioned and forgotten. Not front page.

The boot licking press corps justify their sorry existence by worshipping people who are absent of the academic accomplishments they themselves have achieved. A journalism major shouldn't go brown nose n' the thumb sucking (c-at best, student) nose picker with halted reading and zero aptitude for mathematics.

And the worshipping public? Proves people will buy whatever you sell em'. The entertainment TV and magazine junkies fall in-between the "in the closet" worshippers (who at least know that they should be ashamed of themselves) and the groupie types who are just plain silly. Aside from these groupies, (that I just plain don't understand) and the subservient press everyone wants in on the act.

Not just Warhol's benevolent imagining of 15 minutes of fame for everyone. No! People want it all and are willing to hire a publicist to get it.

Now don't ask how yours truly came to be involved with a publicist just understand this; what a liar! What a dung shoveling liar. A real nobody. Now I'm mindful of the fact that many publicist are good. Look at what we're talking about here. The absent English class celebrity corps need someone to deal with the dweebie press corps. Also media relations and promotions for everything from restaurants, banks, night clubs, broadcast companies and just about anything else;

accept me. I'm not one to fake myself out like that.

However I find myself in an agreement with a P.R. firm. Keep in mind my venture was already getting good press on it's own merit. Coming into the most important season for me, It seemed like a good idea as it was presented to me.

Not only did this, "professional publicist" fail to generate one single thing; because I yielded to them as per our agreement, they killed the on-going publicity.

Lying every step of the way. Used every excuse in the book (sick relative blah blah) to explain why after they'd gotten what I now consider stolen merchandise, they seemed to always be tied up.

Get a load of this story. "I've been so busy because one of my clients is the family of a little boy who is lost in the wilderness". (of Idaho or somewhere). Now ask yourself, why would a family with a child in the wilderness of the north-west United States take the time to contact a New York City P.R.

firm and consummate an agreement with that firm to deal with the press necessary to rescue the kid?..... Huh?

The boy would be dead. Besides I think the family would call the local authorities that are in place for such emergencies. There was no national news on the situation. This woman couldn't come up with a better lie than that? You should have a rehearsed group of stock lies when you're in such a B.S.n' business.

Our introductory meeting should have said it all. We met at a very chic restaurant that her firm represents. (free food). Good enough. She too was impressive. Tall, stylish, attractive young woman. Sparkling personality and wit. Seemed capable of moving mountains.

Then her partner/husband showed up. Five feet even. I sat and wondered momentarily where in heavens name did he find the vat of urine he appeared to have dunked himself into. A Zero! His t-shirt

HI
I'M
VANESSA
THE
WAKEMAN
AGENCY
ME TOO

should have read, my smart wife takes care of me.

Wet kissing booty grabbers on a busy street I'll bet cha'. I should've known as soon as I met him that she'd come up way short. Not a pun, it's a dig. A business partner of mine arrived last. The guy's one of those personal training fitness nuts. A combination of Jack LaLanne and that juice guy. This inspires shorty to announce, he'd thought about becoming a fitness trainer. (pregnant pause).... Might I suggest a bath.

Three and a half months later I was introduced via conference call to my rep. By now I'm pissed enough to write my girls name and number on bathroom walls and she hooks me up with a person who boasts of being from a long line of failures. No joke! Three brothers, Mayflower, two prosper, one bum. Guess which one she comes from. Apples don't fall far from the tree.

If you know any ambulance chasing type of attorney's who'd take this one pro-bono, e-mail me at the publishers e-mail address in front of the book.

This crew qualifies for the, $3 bill of the year award. And with the fees these P.R. firms charge, I'm thinking of hanging a shingle before I get out of here. All you need are the yellow pages. Success isn't guaranteed. Kind of like a stockbroker minus the license and the knowledge required to get licensed. Oh and, I'm gonna make you a star so have your people contact my people and yakity, yakity, yakity, yakity.......ect. ect. ect....plop, plop.

Chapter 18

The "In" Crowd

Between Wall street, T.V. land, the "Art World" and the other stops along the yellow brick road I've seen it all or damn near. Everybody wants to be the "IN" crowd. (Nose blowers. Restaurant nose blowers all of em').

The richer they are, the more they think it. Fine art, fine wine, fine dining and out with the snot rag. (In many ways).

Example: I've got these friends who are the epitome of "high flyers". Hubby & wife team. Or vice versa. They manage one of the premier and now infamous Hedge Funds in the country. Now before the infamy they were pretty cool people. An appreciation for jazz and art.

This is how I met them. They took an interest in my paintings. Bought em'. An artist needs nothing more than a wealthy patron. Remember, their friends and associates are also rich. Not that I'm viewing them that way but let's keep it real.

They didn't quite get it, but good people.

They'd invite me to the intimate staff x-mas parties. Wine, cheese, gifts etc. (I ended up giving them more paintings than they bought). This past x-mas the party was a little different. It was a Christmas prayer. O.K.. No wine. No problem I don't drink. Their minor minister was there to perform this prayer that never happened. I say minor minister because they proudly showed me a photograph taken of them with their major minister. That, "I have sinned against you", guy. (they're pay n' him I'll bet).

This prayer was really a; 'see, here's our tall friend we've been telling you about'. Now there were other people there, obviously to meet the tall friend they'd heard about. Had this been to promote my art the stars would've been aligned.

As I'd been suspecting, they don't display my work to promote me. They show my work to promote themselves. When their super-rich clients or prospects visit, they take them on the grand tour proudly proclaiming their support of a tall artist who they consider a friend. What tipped me off to this was my own grand tour after re-modeling.

Ms. Thang proudly showed off the family coat of arms. The Robert E. Lee family coat of arms. (The women's first name is, 'E. Lee').

Getting back to the prayer party. The preacher-man (see chapter 12) said to me toward the end of the prayer session that never happened that we'd come together for a reason. Essentially he felt that it was "MY" lucky day. That's until I phoned him a few days later and called him everything but a child of god. Then I called my billionaire buddy to offer the same sentiment and demand the return of a significant and highly valued painting that they didn't pay for.

I rent paintings to many companies. They're the only ones who don't pay a monthly fee and they're by far the richest. They're fired. They're not even allowed to buy paintings from me any more. Find another ticket to heaven.

Now I will say that I know 2006 was a very tough year for them. Remember the "infamy" I'd mentioned? Well these ego driven darlings of the world of high finance get themselves caught up in a multi-billion dollar scam. They'll scream from roof tops that they did nothing wrong. So why have they paid a cool one in legal fees to fight the millions or billions in law suits.

Not that I matter but I'd been giving them the benefit of the doubt until that x-mas performance. There's a problem. Well, wifey started her career in penny stocks. Let em' mark 06' as the year they lost the trust of many. I ain't your tall friend.

Fifty people work there and none of them are tall. Go figure.

But for the record, the "Art World" has the most $3 bills. Not the artist, the ones trying to steal the artists money and the phonies pretending they can afford it.
$!@% em' all.

Chapter 19

The War Of The Sexes

It started at the big bang. Mars, Venus, Whatever. Men and Women are different, period. We're not suppose to be the same. That's the way nature planned it. And as long as I live chivalry will never die. And, "that's" the way nature planned it. Chivalry not chauvinism.

This is no place to be too serious but women are oppressed and abused all over the world. Discriminated against at the very least. This beastly fact alone proves we're just monkeys with car keys.

Women are slightly advanced in terms of social development, want proof? We guys pee in bathroom sinks and don't know why. Men are also more likely to cross those you know what lines. And it's disgusting. This has nothing to do with sexuality. It's more about domain, territory.

The lines are not crystal clear, but here's a place to start.......

Sugar & Spice & Everything Nice	Snakes & Snails & Puppydog Tails
Girls	Boys
Earrings, Jewelry	Football
Nail salons	Basketball
Hair Salons	Baseball
Anything Salons	Strip Joints
Oprah	Tacky Jokes
Fluted Glasses	Beer
Gossip	Combat Boots
Cigarette holders	Combat
Bonding	Pipe Smoking
Ballet	Cigars
Modeling	Public Nastiness
Pink	If we build it, they will come
Cosmetics	Trinkets
Paying Bills On Time	Athletes Foot Fungus
Leotards	Packing & Lifting
Fur Coats	Yard work
Diamond Rings	Trash Collecting
Housework	Losing The Argument on Purpose
Cheerleading	Not having a Clue
De-caff	Skipping the Shower
Lightly toasted	Peeing in the sink
Just because	DoDo n' away from home

Chapter 20

The Media

Punk-ass. Don't make me come down there !!
Ya' punk-ass.

Chapter 21

Religion

Just two points here.....

Point #1 Religion seems to make some people crazy.

Point #2 I'd be atheist if I wasn't scared of God.

Chapter 22

Just For The Record

It's a good thing Babe Ruth could hit, because he sure as hell couldn't run.

Good thing Jimi Hendrix could play a guitar, because he sure as hell couldn't sing.

There's no such thing as a high class strip joint or a high class hooker no matter how much patrons pay for drinks or whatever. I'm not dissin' the world's oldest hustle. I'm saying your clientele is grimy. Sneaky and grimy.

Carrots are good for you. (you had to be there).

Oprah's hot!

I'm Kid Shelleen.

The Government sucks.

Hef is "Da Man"!

Darnell is a genius (heredity).

There ain't no Santa Claus.

There ain't no UFOs or aliens.

The fungus is among us.

Damn the Republicans.

Damn the Democrats.

Damn Uncle Sam.

Desperately seeking Cat Ballou.

I think I picked the wrong one (you had to be there).

The angry voices in my head are from Outer Space.

Mona Lisa was a man.

Jackie Mason is a nobody. (See, you don't even know who I'm talking about).

Mary rained down from heaven. (not that Mary you religious fool).

Math is easy.

Exit Stage Left

I'm not asking for company but I've noticed I'm not the only one who could use a looong vacation. Here's the scene that underscored my conclusion.

One afternoon I was in a smallish but chic coffee shop. Looking around I noticed a few people sat alone like myself. At least two of these people were talking to themselves not unlike myself. Full blown conversations. The difference was that the other nuts didn't care who looked at them or how others looked at them. I still try to hide my craziness.

That's how I know the train is in the station. Enough! Got some baby bulls in that last litter. It ain't retirement time but I'm sending these little cows to market. That means it's time to go somewhere to hide the loot. The lying government ain't getting it. I'm taking my marbles and going home. I'm a 100% entrepreneur! Already there are a dozen hands in the proverbial pot. Let them pay the government.

And why'd she leave me? She, she and she? ….taxes…winter weather….

So I'll be chasing summer now. When it leaves I'll go with it. I've paid my dues. I've paid dues for my next ten generations. So I gotta go paint. Those generations get to cash in on my pain after I'm dead. So that's me walking off into the sunset, easel in tow. The girl from Ipanema went that-a-way.

Ray Tempus Books

· A 40 Point Guide To Peeing In New York

*** Last One Gone Turn The Lights Out**

Next

· Phony As A Three Dollar Bill

www.40points.com

...... in parting

To those of you with
whom I must deal;
... DON'T MAKE MY NEXT BOOK !!